Margo and Marky's Adventures in Reading

by Thomas Kingsley Troupe

illustrated by Natalia Vasquez

PICTURE WINDOW BOOKS
a capstone imprint

Thanks to our adviser for his expertise, research, and advice:

Terry Flaherty, PhD, Professor of English
Minnesota State University, Mankato

Editor: **Shelly Lyons**
Designer: **Lori Bye**
Art Director: **Nathan Gassman**
Production Specialist: **Sarah Bennett**
The illustrations in this book were created digitally.

Picture Window Books
151 Good Counsel Drive
P.O. Box 669
Mankato, MN 56002-0669
877-845-8392
www.capstonepub.com

Library of Congress Cataloging-in-Publication Data
Troupe, Thomas Kingsley.
Margo and Marky's adventures in reading / by Thomas Kingsley Troupe ;
illustrated by Natalia Vasquez.
    p. cm. – (In the library)
  Includes bibliographical references and index.
  ISBN 978-1-4048-6291-3 (library binding)
  1. Books and reading–Juvenile literature. I. Vasquez, Natalia, ill.
II. Title.
  Z1003.T76 2011

028.5'5–dc22   2010026899

Printed in the United States of America in North Mankato, Minnesota.
072011   006241R

This is Margo and her bookmark, Marky. They're world-class adventurers who travel to faraway lands. They meet interesting people and learn cool stuff. And they do it all from the library.

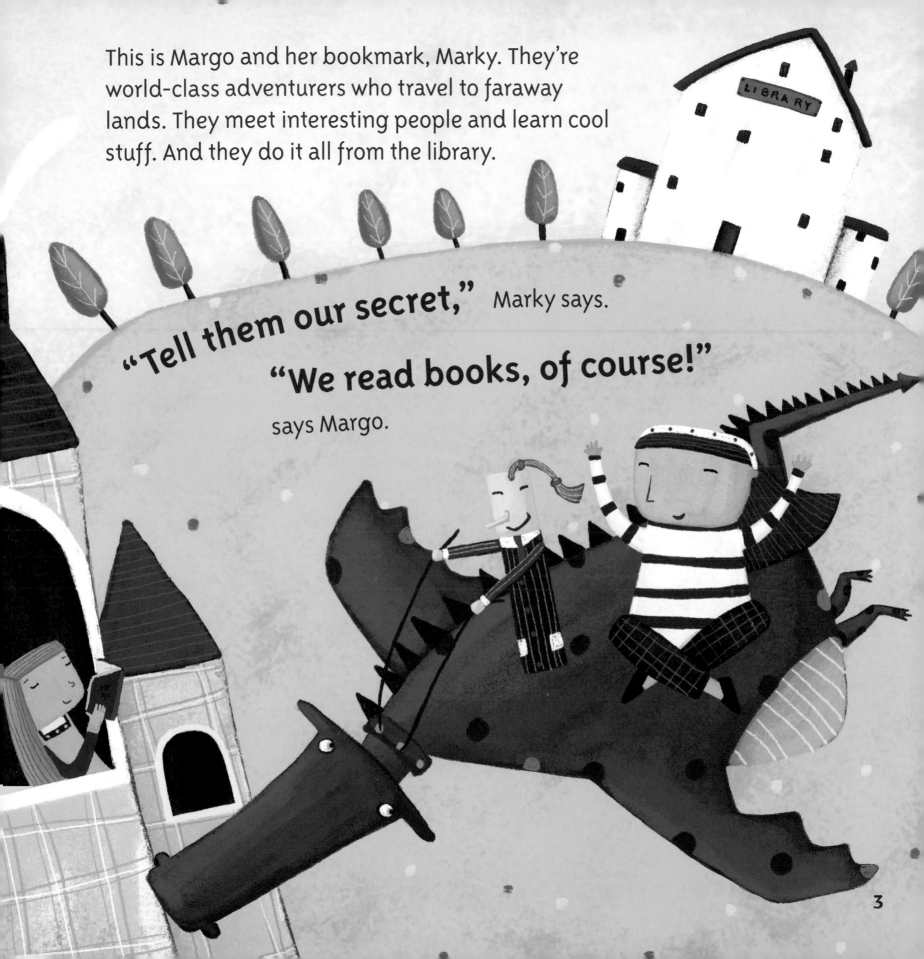

"Tell them our secret," Marky says.

"We read books, of course!" says Margo.

3

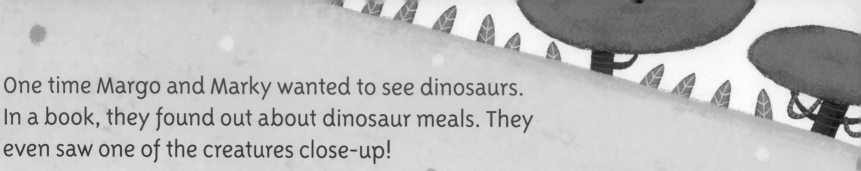

One time Margo and Marky wanted to see dinosaurs. In a book, they found out about dinosaur meals. They even saw one of the creatures close-up!

"It was like we were there!" Marky says.

"A **Tyrannosaurus rex** stomped through the jungle," Margo says. "It was looking for something to eat. Marky and I ran. Then we ducked into a small cave. It was a close call!"

"I can still smell the T.-rex's breath," Marky says.

5

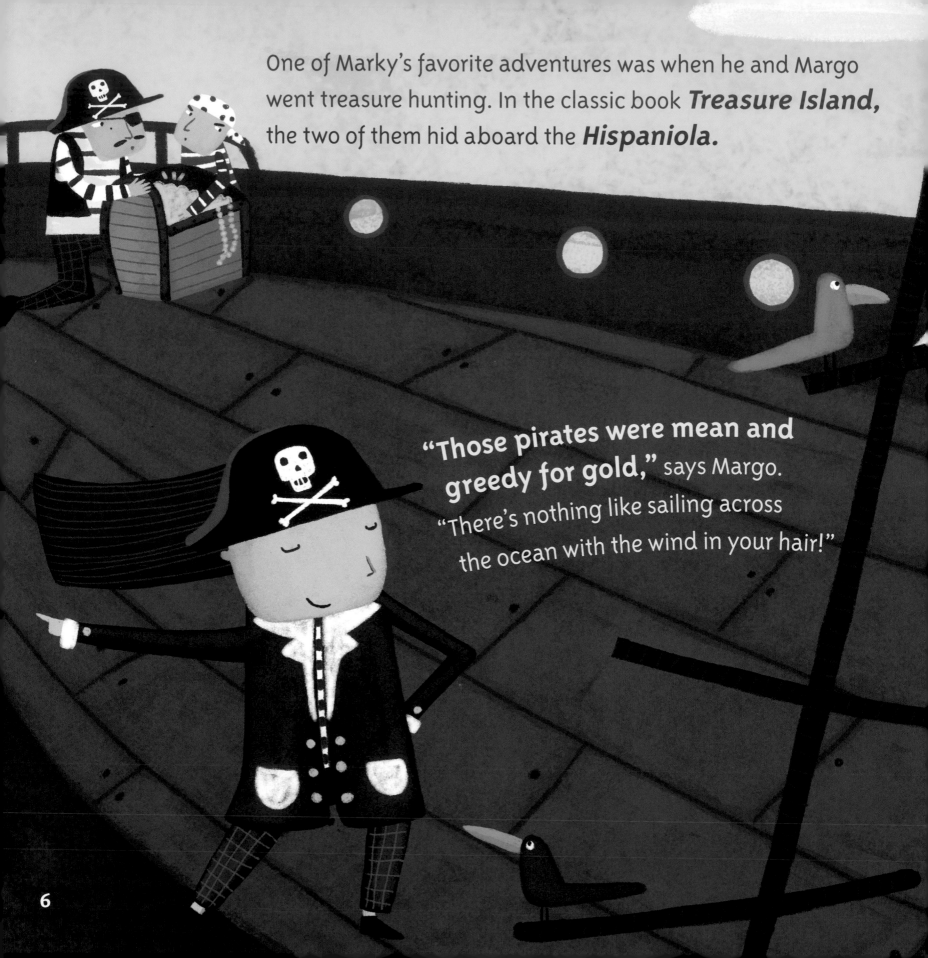

One of Marky's favorite adventures was when he and Margo went treasure hunting. In the classic book **Treasure Island,** the two of them hid aboard the **Hispaniola.**

"Those pirates were mean and greedy for gold," says Margo. "There's nothing like sailing across the ocean with the wind in your hair!"

6

"**Arrrr,**" Marky says. "X marks the spot!"

"**And you mark the page,**" Margo jokes. "Those nasty pirates were in for a real surprise! I won't tell you what happened when **Long John Silver's crew** dug for the treasure. You should read it yourself."

Not every book Margo and
Marky read is action-packed.
Sometimes learning how to do
new things is an adventure.

"With help from my parents
and a great book, we built
a **birdhouse,**" says Margo.
"The local birds loved it!"

"We should build a **bird hotel** next time!" Marky says.

"Or maybe even a **bird city**," Margo replies.

Fly Right Inn

Books can teach you how to do just about anything. Cooking, exercise, writing ... you name it. That's the power of books!

9

Have you ever wanted to go on tour with a **rock band?** Margo and Marky did. So they found books about it! Reading about real-life musicians was just like being with them. It almost felt like being on stage.

"My ears are still ringing from the **guitars,**" Marky says.

"You don't have ears," Margo reminds him.

"Oh, yeah," Marky says.

A book about a real person is called a biography. It tells the story of that person's life. When someone writes about his or her own life, the book is called an autobiography.

Have you ever wished you could travel as fast as the speed of sound? Margo and Marky have. They found a book about jet planes.

BOOOM!

"Remember the time we flew across the sky in a **supersonic jet?**" Marky asks.

"**I sure do!**" answers Margo. "I held on tight and couldn't believe the view. **Reading can be a wild ride!**"

"You jumped when you heard the huge **BOOM,**" Marky says.

Not sure how to speak Greek? Neither were Margo and Marky, before their adventure in language. They found a book that taught them how to speak Greek. It was a blast learning how to write the letters in the Greek alphabet.

"Η ανάγνωση είναι διασκέδαση!"
(EE ah-NAH-gnoh-see EE-neh thee-ah-SKEH-dah-see) Marky says.

"That means 'reading is fun,' "
Margo says.

"Yes," says Marky. "So many adventures begin within the pages of a book."

"We should learn Japanese next," Margo says.

Learning about your own body can be an adventure. Margo and Marky discovered how blood moves through arteries. There are tons of books that explain how the human body works. Margo and Marky found books about the heart, lungs, and brain. They even found out how toenails grow!

"Blood moves through arteries in waves," Marky says.

"We looked at pictures and saw what blood is made of," says Margo. "Reading about blood made us curious about the heart too. Books can take you from one adventure to another!"

Margo and Marky found a book on the human body with the help of a librarian. Remember, librarians are there to help you, so be sure to ask them for suggestions and help when needed.

Margo and Marky love movies almost as much as books. They wondered who invented movies. Before Margo and Marky knew it, they were hanging out with Thomas Edison. He invented the kinetoscope and lots of other things.

phonograph

18

"It's amazing how many **inventions** Edison created," Margo says.

"Margo, do you know what Edison enjoyed when he wasn't **experimenting?**" Marky asks.

"No," Margo replies. **"What?"**

"Reading!" Marky shouts.

kinetoscope

19

No adventure would be complete without reading some of the most popular children's books ever written. Margo and Marky helped Charlotte spin her famous web. They discovered life on the prairie with Laura Ingalls Wilder. They even visited Wonka's wacky chocolate factory with Charlie.

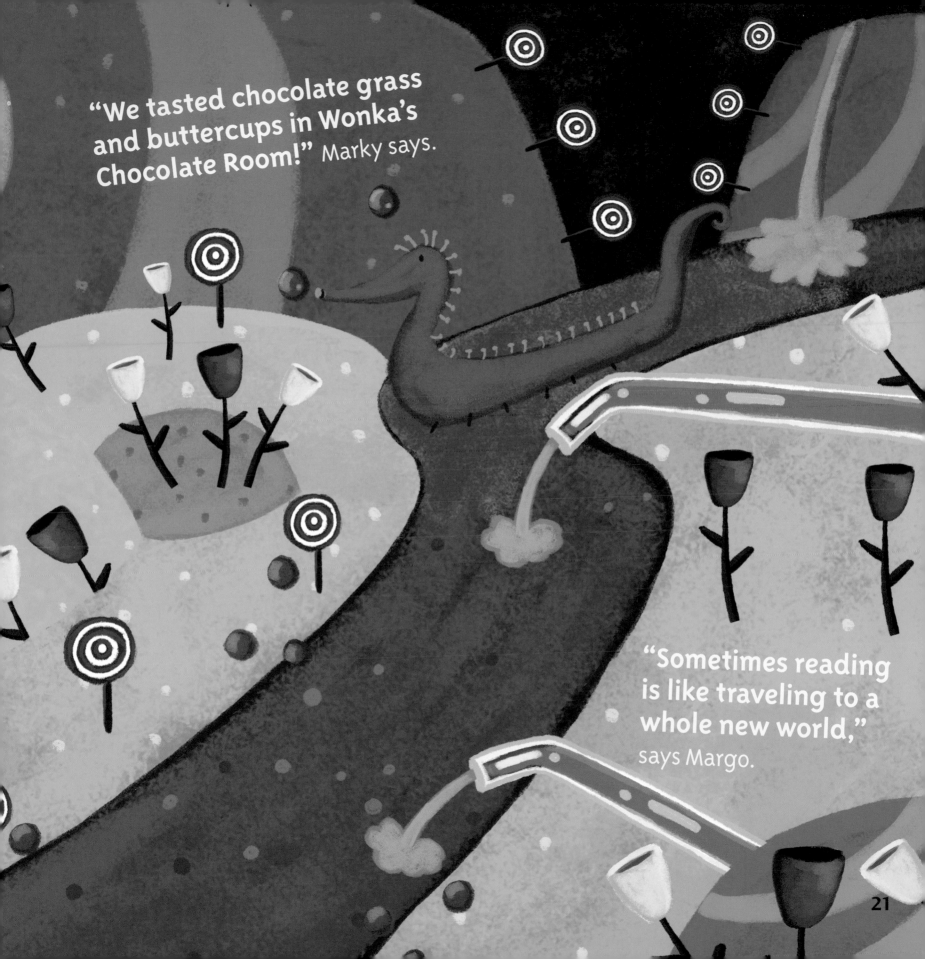

"We tasted chocolate grass and buttercups in Wonka's Chocolate Room!" Marky says.

"Sometimes reading is like traveling to a whole new world," says Margo.

21

"There are **billions of books!**"
Marky says.

"When you **keep reading,**
the **adventures never end!**" says Margo.

Of course, **you** too can be an adventurer like Margo
and Marky. All you need is your **imagination** and
a **quiet place to read.**

GLOSSARY

artery—a tube that carries blood away from the heart to all parts of the body

experiment—to test to learn something new

greedy—wanting more than is needed

invent—to think up and make something new

invention—a new idea or machine

kinetoscope—an early motion picture device; images were viewed through a peephole

supersonic—faster than the speed of sound

MORE BOOKS TO READ

Buzzeo, Toni. *The Library Doors.* Fort Atkinson, Wis.: Upstart Books, 2008.

Finn, Carrie. *Manners in the Library.* Way to Be! Minneapolis: Picture Window Books, 2007.

Terry, Sonya. *"L" Is for Library.* Fort Atkinson, Wis.: Upstart Books, 2006.

INTERNET SITES

FactHound offers a safe, fun way to find Internet sites related to this book. All of the sites on FactHound have been researched by our staff.

Here's all you do:

Visit *www.facthound.com*

Type in this code: 9781404862913

 **Super-cool stuff!** Check out projects, games and lots more at **www.capstonekids.com**

INDEX

LOOK FOR ALL OF THE BOOKS IN THE IN THE LIBRARY SERIES:

* Bob the Alien Discovers the Dewey Decimal System

* Bored Bella Learns About Fiction and Nonfiction

* Karl and Carolina Uncover the Parts of a Book

* Margo and Marky's Adventures in Reading

* Pingpong Perry Experiences How a Book Is Made

* Quinn and Penny Investigate How to Research